Finance Basics

2Ơ MINUTE MANAGER SERIES

Get up to speed fast on essential business skills. Whether you're looking for a crash course or a brief refresher, you'll find just what you need in HBR's 20-Minute Manager series—foundational reading for ambitious professionals and aspiring executives. Each book is a concise, practical primer, so you'll have time to brush up on a variety of key management topics.

Advice you can quickly read and apply, from the most trusted source in business.

Titles include:

Creating Business Plans

Delegating Work

Finance Basics

Managing Projects

Managing Time

Managing Up

Presentations

Running Meetings

20 MINUTE MANAGER SERIES

Finance Basics

Decode the jargon
Navigate key statements
Gauge performance

HARVARD BUSINESS REVIEW PRESS

Boston, Massachusetts

The web addresses referenced in this book were live and correct at
the time of the book's publication but may be subject to change.

Library of Congress Cataloging-in-Publication Data

Finance basics.
    pages cm. — (20-minute manager series)

    1. Corporations—Finance.   2. Managerial accounting.
    HG4026.F487 2014
    658.15—dc23

                                        2013039035

    ISBN: 9781633695771
    eISBN: 9781625270894

Preview

No matter where you work in your organization, you'll do your job better if you understand basic financial concepts. You'll be a more effective contributor to your company's efforts to make money and grow.

This short book explains the basics of finance. Though reading it won't make you a finance expert, it will help you:

- Make sense of the three key financial statements.

- Gauge your company's financial health.

- Weigh costs and benefits before committing resources.

- Consider financial risks when making decisions.

- Estimate future performance.

- Track investments against what you've budgeted.

Contents

Contents

Contents

Finance Basics

Why Understand Finance?

Why Understand Finance?

Finance matters to all companies because they all have to bring in money and spend it in order to do business. On the bringing-in side, smart managers consider questions like these:

- How much of our money comes from the owners? How much from sales? How much from borrowing?

- Which of our product lines and regions earn the highest profits? Which ones fail to perform?

- How long does it take to collect money that customers owe us?

On the spending side:

- Are our costs what they should be? Are we spending the right amount on our people and on our physical assets, such as office space and computer equipment?

- If we can invest in only one of several opportunities for growth, how do we determine which one would generate the most value?

- If we increased our output by 20%, would we make 20% more money?

Your company's finance department (or bookkeeper, if it's a very small company) produces financial statements, budgets, and forecasts. By understanding these documents, you'll gain the information you need to ask essential questions and make smart decisions for your division, department, or team.

By the way, finance uses jargon that may be unfamiliar to you. Sometimes different terms mean exactly the same thing—*profit* and *earnings*, for example, or *sales* and *revenue*. If you're not certain what a term means, just look it up in the "Key Terms" section at the end of this book.

Navigating the Three Major Financial Statements

Navigating the Three Major Financial Statements

T he underlying purpose of every company is to make money. So if you're a manager, part of your job is to help your company earn a profit—ideally, a bigger one each year.

Of course, you may work in the nonprofit or government sector, where making money isn't the most important goal. But you will still have to monitor the money that comes in and goes out.

Wherever you work, you can improve the financial health of your organization by reducing costs, increasing revenue, or both. You can help the organization make good investments and use its resources wisely.

The best managers don't just watch the budget—they look for the right combination of controlling costs, improving sales, and utilizing assets more effectively. They understand where revenue comes from, how the money is spent, and how much profit the company is making. They know how good a job the company is doing at turning *profit* into *cash*. (No, those are not the same thing. We'll discuss the difference later.)

To learn all this, managers rely primarily on three documents: the income statement, the balance sheet, and the cash flow statement. These are called **financial statements**, or just financials. Publicly traded companies—those that sell stock to the public on an exchange—make summary financial statements available to everyone, usually on a quarterly basis. Privately held companies—owned by one person, a family, or a small group of investors—often keep their financial statements private. But nearly every company produces detailed financials for internal use.

Accounting methods

You don't have to be an accountant to understand finance. But you do have to know just a couple of important things about accounting.

First, financial statements follow the same general format from one company to another. Individual line items may vary somewhat, depending on the nature of the business. But the statements are usually similar enough that you can easily compare performance. The reason for the similarity is that accountants all follow the same set of rules. In the United States, those rules are called **generally accepted accounting principles**, or GAAP (pronounced "gap").

Second, GAAP allows two different methods of accounting. **Cash-based accounting** is typically used by very small companies. It's really simple. The company records a sale whenever it receives cash for a product or a service and records an expense whenever it issues a check.

The other method, **accrual accounting**, is a little more complicated and far more common. The company records a sale whenever it delivers a product or a service, not when cash changes hands. (That might be a month or two later, when the customer pays the bill.) It records an expense whenever it *incurs* one, not when it actually writes a check. The key to this method is what accountants call the matching principle: *Match every cost to the revenue that is associated with it.*

Let's look at an example. Amalgamated Hat Rack, an imaginary company that manufactures hat racks from imitation moose antlers, records revenue each time it ships racks to a customer. Because the customer hasn't paid yet, revenue always includes estimates of cash the company will receive in the future.

When Amalgamated orders 2,000 brass hooks from a supplier, it doesn't record the expense of those hooks all at once; rather, it records part of the expense *with every sale*. If each hat rack has five brass hooks, the accountants record the cost of five brass hooks every time one hat rack is sold.

Why use the accrual method? Because it gives you a more accurate picture of profit. If you work for a hat rack company, you want to know whether each hat rack you sell is profitable. To answer that question, you have to track the costs you incur and the revenue you bring in every time you make one and ship it to a customer.

The income statement

The income statement tells you whether the company is making a profit—that is, whether it has positive net income—according to the rules of accrual accounting. (*Income* is just another word for *profit*, which is why the income statement is also called a profit-and-loss statement, or P&L.) It shows a company's revenue, expenses, and profit or loss for a specific period of time—typically a month, a quarter, or a year.

How does an income statement present this profit picture? It begins with the company's revenue or total net sales (same thing) during the period it covers. It then lists all the various costs, including the cost of making the goods or delivering the services, overhead expenses, taxes, and so on, and subtracts them from revenue. The bottom line—what's left over—is the net income, or profit. (See figure 1, "Amalgamated Hat Rack income statement.")

Let's look more closely at the line items that appear on the income statement. **Cost of goods sold** (usually abbreviated as COGS) is what it cost Amalgamated to manufacture the hat racks. That includes raw materials, labor, and any other costs directly related to production.

Subtract COGS from revenue and you get **gross profit**, which shows how much the company made before paying its overhead, taxes, and so on. You can use this number to calculate **gross margin**, which doesn't appear on the income statement but is still an important number. Just divide gross profit by

FIGURE 1

Amalgamated Hat Rack income statement

	For the period ending December 31, 2013	
Retail sales	$ 2,200,000	
Corporate sales	1,000,000	
Total sales revenue	3,200,000	
Less: Cost of goods sold	1,600,000	
Gross profit	1,600,000	
Less: Operating expenses	800,000	
Less: Depreciation expenses	42,500	
Earnings before interest and taxes	757,500	
Less: Interest expense	110,000	
Earnings before income taxes	647,500	
Less: Income taxes	300,000	
Net income	$ 347,500	

revenue. Amalgamated Hat Rack's gross margin is $1.6 million divided by $3.2 million, or 50%.

Operating expenses—also known as sales, general, and administrative expenses (SG&A), or simply overhead—include the salaries of administrative employees, rents, sales and marketing expenses, and any other cost not directly attributed to manufacturing a product or delivering a service. The cost of the company's phone system, for example, would be included on this line.

Depreciation is a way of estimating the cost of assets that last a relatively long time. A computer system, for example, might have a useful life of three years. So it doesn't make sense to record its entire cost in the first year. Rather, the company spreads the expense over the system's useful life. If the accountants employ a simple straight-line method of depreciation, they would record one-third of the total cost on the company's income statement each year.

Subtract operating expenses and depreciation from gross profit and you get **operating income**, often called **earnings before interest and taxes**, or **EBIT**. Subtract interest costs and taxes from EBIT and you get **net income**, or profit—the famous bottom line.

The balance sheet

A balance sheet is a snapshot: It summarizes a company's financial position at a given point in time, usually the last day of a year or a quarter. It shows what the company *owns* (its **assets**), what it *owes* (its **liabilities**), and the difference between them, called **owners' equity** or **shareholders' equity**.

A balance sheet is called that because it always balances. That is, all the assets must equal all the liabilities plus owners' equity. This is sometimes known as the fundamental accounting equation, and it looks like this:

Assets = liabilities + owners' equity

Here's why the equation holds true.

Assets are everything a company owns. The category includes cash, land, buildings, vehicles, machinery, computers, and even intangible assets such as patents. (It doesn't include people, because the company doesn't own its employees.)

Of course, a company has to acquire these assets. It can use its own money, which is the money its owners have invested in it plus the money the company itself has earned over time. Or it can use borrowed money. In balance sheet terminology, its own money is owners' equity, and borrowed funds are liabilities.

And because you can't get something for nothing, the assets need to equal liabilities plus owners' equity. If a company has $3 million in assets and $2 million in liabilities, it must have owners' equity of $1 million.

Balance sheet data are most helpful when compared with information from a previous year. In figure 2, "Amalgamated Hat Rack balance sheet as of December 31, 2013 and 2012," a comparison of the figures for 2013 against those for 2012 shows that

FIGURE 2

Amalgamated Hat Rack balance sheet as of December 31, 2013 and 2012

	2013	2012	Increase (Decrease)
Assets			
Cash and marketable securities	$ 652,500	486,500	166,000
Accounts receivable	555,000	512,000	43,000
Inventory	835,000	755,000	80,000
Prepaid expenses	123,000	98,000	25,000
Total current assets	2,165,500	1,851,500	314,000
Gross property, plant, and equipment	2,100,000	1,900,000	200,000
Less: accumulated depreciation	333,000	290,500	(42,500)
Net property, plant, and equipment	1,767,000	1,609,500	157,500
Total assets	$ 3,932,500	3,461,000	471,500
Liabilities and owners' equity			
Accounts payable	$ 450,000	430,000	20,000
Accrued expenses	98,000	77,000	21,000
Income tax payable	17,000	9,000	8,000
Short-term debt	435,000	500,000	(65,000)
Total current liabilities	1,000,000	1,016,000	(16,000)
Long-term debt	750,000	660,000	90,000
Total liabilities	1,750,000	1,676,000	74,000
Contributed capital	900,000	850,000	50,000
Retained earnings	1,282,500	935,000	347,500
Total owners' equity	2,182,500	1,785,000	397,500
Total liabilities and owners' equity	$ 3,932,500	$ 3,461,000	$ 471,500

Amalgamated has increased its total liabilities by $74,000 and its total assets by $471,500, resulting in an increase in owners' equity.

Again, let's look more closely at the terms. The balance sheet begins by listing the most liquid assets: *cash and marketable securities,* **accounts receivable** (what customers owe as of the balance sheet's date), and *inventory,* along with any costs that have been paid in advance (**prepaid expenses**). These are called **current assets**. Next it tallies assets that are less liquid—for example, buildings and machinery, known as **property, plant, and equipment** (**PPE**). These are called **fixed assets** or **long-term assets**.

Companies value their fixed assets according to what the assets originally cost. But because all fixed assets (other than land) depreciate over time, the accountants must also include any depreciation on those assets that they have recorded so far on income statements. Gross property, plant, and equipment minus accumulated depreciation equals **net property,**

TIP: SHORT-TERM DEBT

The balance sheet distinguishes between short- and long-term debt. Short-term debt must be paid in a year or less. It includes accounts payable, short-term notes, salaries, and income taxes.

---

plant, and equipment—in other words, the current **book value** of the company's fixed assets.

The line items under liabilities and owners' equity are pretty easy to understand. **Accounts payable** is what the company owes its suppliers; **income tax payable** is what it owes the government. **Accrued expenses** are funds owed for salaries or other costs not included under accounts payable. **Short-term debt** is debt that must be paid in less than a year.

These are the company's **current liabilities**. Subtracting current liabilities from current assets gives you what's known as **working capital**, which indicates how much money the company has tied up in operating activities. So for 2013, Amalgamated had $2,165,500 minus $1,000,000, or $1,165,500, in working capital.

Most long-term liabilities are loans of one sort or another, so the balance sheet shows long-term debt and then **total liabilities**, which is just the sum of current and long-term liabilities. **Owners' equity**, as we have seen, is the total of what shareholders have invested in the company over time (**contributed capital**) and what it has earned and retained in past years (**retained earnings**).

The cash flow statement

A cash flow statement gives you a peek into a company's checking account. Like a bank statement, it tells how much cash was on hand at the beginning of a period and how much at the end. It also shows where the cash came from and how the company spent it.

If you work for a large corporation, changes in the company's cash flow probably don't affect your daily work. Still, it's a good idea to stay up-to-date with the cash flow statement and projections, because they may come into play when you prepare your budget for the coming year. If cash is tight, you will probably be asked to spend conservatively. If it's plentiful, you may have opportunities to make new investments. The same goes for small companies, of course, where cash is often very tight. Even if the company is profitable, owners may sometimes wonder whether they can make payroll.

The cash flow statement shows how well your company is turning profits into cash, and that ability is ultimately what keeps a business solvent. We see in figure 3, "Amalgamated Hat Rack cash flow statement for the year ending December 31, 2013," that the company generated a net increase in cash of $166,000 in 2013. Note that this is *not* the same as net profit, which is shown on the income statement as $347,500. The

FIGURE 3

Amalgamated Hat Rack cash flow statement for the year ending December 31, 2013

Net income	$ 347,500
Operating activities	
Accounts receivable	(43,000)
Inventory	(80,000)
Prepaid expenses	(25,000)
Accounts payable	20,000
Accrued expenses	21,000
Income tax payable	8,000
Depreciation expenses	42,500
Total changes in operating assets and liabilities	(56,500)
Cash flow from operations	291,000
Investing activities	
Sale of property, plant, and equipment	267,000*
Capital expenditures	(467,000)
Cash flow from investing activities	(200,000)
Financing activities	
Short-term debt decrease	(65,000)
Long-term borrowing	90,000
Capital stock	50,000
Cash dividends to stockholders	—
Cash flow from financing activities	75,000
Increase in cash during year	$ 166,000

* Assumes sale price was at book value; the company had yet to start depreciating this asset.

income statement includes depreciation and other items that do not involve any cash. It records revenue and expenses as they are incurred rather than when cash changes hands. The cash flow statement shows investments in capital assets such as machinery that show up on the income statement only as those assets are depreciated.

Notice, however, that the cash flow statement starts with net income and, through a series of adjustments, translates that into net cash. For instance, it adds depreciation back in, because depreciation is an expense that involves no cash. (You don't need to worry about the technicalities, but if you're interested, there are many books that explain the process. See "Learn More" at the end of this book.)

Again, let's look at some key terms. The first big category is **cash flow from operations**. That just means all the cash the company took in or spent on ongoing operations—cash from customers, cash spent on wages and materials, and so on. A company's operating cash flow is a very good indicator of its financial health. If it's negative, the company may be in serious trouble. (A negative number on a cash flow statement is indicated by parentheses.)

The second big category is **cash flow from investing activities**. "Investing" in this context means money spent on assets such as machinery or vehicles and money realized from the sale of such equipment. For most companies, cash from investing activities should be a negative number. That means the company is investing some of its cash in assets that will generate future growth.

The third big category is **cash flow from financing activities**. This includes any cash received from a company's owners (shareholders) or paid to its owners in the form of dividends. It also includes cash received from loans and cash paid to lenders.

Add up all three major categories and you get the **increase in cash during the year**. Of course, for some companies, it might be a decrease, particularly if the company is growing fast and investing heavily in capital assets. This figure corresponds to the increase or decrease in cash and marketable securities that appears at the top of a two-year balance sheet comparison.

Using the
Statements
to Measure
Financial Health

Using the Statements to Measure Financial Health

The financial statements tell different but related stories about how well your company is doing financially:

- The income statement shows the bottom line. Using the rules of accounting, it indicates how much profit or loss a company generated over a period of time—a month, a quarter, or a year.

- The balance sheet shows whether a company is solvent. It provides a snapshot of the company's assets, liabilities, and equity on a given day.

- The cash flow statement shows how much cash a company is generating. It also tracks, in broad terms, where that cash came from and what it is being used for.

Now you're ready to take the next step: interpreting the numbers these statements provide. For example, is the company's profit large or small? Is its level of debt healthy or unhealthy? You can answer such questions through ratio analysis.

A financial ratio is just two numbers from the financial statements expressed in relation to each other. The ratios that follow are useful for almost any industry. But if you want to gauge your own company's performance, the most meaningful comparison is usually with other companies in the same industry.

Profitability ratios

Profitability ratios help you evaluate a company's profitability by expressing its profit as a percentage of something else. They include:

- *Return on sales (ROS)*, or net income divided by revenue. (Remember that net income on the income statement just means profit.) Also known as **net profit margin**, ROS measures how much profit the company earns as a percentage of every sales dollar. For example, if a company makes a profit of $10 for every $100 in sales, the ROS is 10/100, or 10%.

- *Return on assets (ROA)*, or net income divided by total assets. (You can find total assets on the balance sheet.) ROA indicates how efficiently the company is using its assets to generate profit.

- ***Return on equity (ROE)***, or net income divided by owners' equity. ROE shows how much profit the company is generating as a percentage of the owners' investment.

- ***Gross profit margin***, or gross profit divided by revenue. This ratio reflects the profitability of the company's products or services without considering overhead or other expenses.

- ***Earnings before interest and taxes (EBIT) margin***, or operating profit divided by revenue. Many analysts use this indicator, also known as operating margin, to see how profitable a company's operating activities are.

You can use these ratios to compare one company with another and to track your own company's performance over time. A profitability ratio that is headed in the wrong direction is usually a sign of trouble.

Efficiency ratios

Efficiency ratios show you how efficiently a company is managing its assets and liabilities. They include:

- *Asset turnover,* or revenue divided by total assets. The higher the number, the better a company is at employing assets to generate revenue.

- *Days sales outstanding,* or ending accounts receivable (from the balance sheet) divided by revenue per day (annual revenue divided by 360). This ratio tells you how long (on average) it takes a company to collect what it's owed. A company that takes 45 days to collect its receivables needs significantly more working capital than one that takes 20 days to collect.

- **_Days payable outstanding_**, or ending accounts payable divided by cost of goods sold per day. This measure tells you how many days it takes a company to pay its suppliers. The more days it takes, the longer a company can use the cash. Of course, the desire for more cash has to be balanced against maintaining good relationships with suppliers.

- **_Inventory days_**, or average inventory divided by cost of goods sold per day. This ratio indicates how long it takes a company to sell the average amount of inventory on hand during a given period of time. The longer it takes, the more cash the company has tied up and the greater the likelihood that the inventory will not be sold at full value.

Again, it's often helpful to compare changes in these ratios from one period to the next, and to track trends in the ratios over three years or more.

Liquidity ratios

Liquidity ratios tell you about a company's ability to meet current financial obligations such as debt payments, payroll, and vendor payments. They include:

- *Current ratio,* or total current assets divided by total current liabilities. This is a prime measure of a company's ability to pay its bills. It's so popular with lenders that it's sometimes called the **banker's ratio**. Generally speaking, a higher ratio indicates greater financial strength than a lower one.

- *Quick ratio,* or current assets minus inventory, with the result divided by current liabilities. This ratio is sometimes called the **acid test**. It measures a company's ability to deal with its liabilities quickly without having to liquidate its inventory.

Lenders aren't the only stakeholders who scrutinize liquidity ratios. Suppliers, too, are likely to inspect them before offering credit terms.

Leverage ratios

Leverage ratios tell you how, and how extensively, a company relies on debt. (The word *leverage* in this context means using debt to finance a business or an investment.)

- *Interest coverage,* or earnings before interest and taxes (EBIT) divided by interest expense. This measures a company's margin of safety: It shows how many times over the company could make its interest payments from its operating profit.

- *Debt to equity,* or total liabilities divided by owners' equity. This shows how much a company has borrowed compared with the money its owners have invested. A high debt-to-equity ratio (relative to other companies in the industry) is sometimes a reason for concern; the company is said to be highly leveraged.

Nearly every company borrows money at some point in its life. Like a household with a mortgage, a company can use debt to finance investments that it otherwise couldn't afford. The debt becomes a problem only when it's too high to be supported.

Other ways to measure financial health

Other methods of assessing a company's financial health include valuation, Economic Value Added (EVA), and measurements of growth and productivity. Like the ratios just discussed, these measures are most meaningful when you are comparing companies in the same industry or looking at one company's performance over time.

Valuation usually refers to the process for determining the total value of a company. The book value is simply the owners' equity figure on the balance sheet. But the market value of the business—what an acquirer would pay for it—may be quite different.

Publicly traded companies can measure their market value every day: They just multiply the daily stock price by the number of shares outstanding. A privately held company—or someone who is considering buying one—must estimate its market value. One method is to estimate future cash flows and then use some interest rate to determine how much that stream of cash is worth right now. A second method is to evaluate the company's assets—both physical assets and intangible assets such as patents or customer lists. A third is to look at the market value of publicly traded companies that are similar to the company being evaluated.

Of course, a company may be worth different amounts to different buyers. If your employer owns

ANALYZING FINANCIAL STATEMENTS

- Compare numbers with what's typical in a given industry.

- Compare statements of similar-sized companies.

- Watch for trends: How have the statements changed since last year? From three years ago?

a unique technology, for instance, an acquirer that wants that technology for its operations may be willing to pay a premium for the business.

Valuation also refers to the process by which Wall Street investors and stock analysts determine what a publicly traded company "ought" to be selling for (in their view). That helps them decide whether the current market price of the stock is a good deal or a bad

one. Analysts and investors use various gauges in this
process, including:

- **_Earnings per share (EPS)_,** or net income
  divided by the number of shares outstanding.
  This is one of the most commonly watched indicators of a company's financial performance.
  If it falls, it will most likely take the stock's price
  down with it.

- **_Price-to-earnings ratio (P/E)_,** or the current
  price of a share of stock divided by the previous
  12 months' earnings per share.

- **_Growth indicators_,** such as the increase in
  revenue, earnings, or earnings per share from
  one year to the next. A company that is growing
  will probably provide increasing returns to its
  shareholders over time.

- **_Economic Value Added (EVA)_.** A registered
  trademark of the consulting firm Stern, Stew-
  art, EVA indicates a company's profitability

after a charge for the cost of capital is deducted. The calculation is quite technical.

- *Productivity measures.* Sales per employee and net income per employee are two measures that link revenue and profit to workforce data. Trend lines in these numbers may suggest greater or lesser operating efficiency over time.

Wall Street loves statistics, and these are just a few of the indicators that the professionals use. But they are among the most common.

Preparing
a Budget

Preparing a Budget

A budget is a financial blueprint for achieving business goals.

Your unit's budget is part of the company's overall strategy, so you need to understand the company's strategy in order to create a useful budget. There are several steps you can take to increase your strategic understanding:

- *Pay attention to communications from senior management.* Most companies try to communicate at least the basics of their strategy to the entire organization.

- *Watch the overall economic picture.* A company's strategy during a recession will differ from its strategy in a booming economy. Listen to your manager's and colleagues' views on sales and the economy, and make your own observations as well. Are you deluged by résumés, or is good help hard to find? Are prices rising or falling?

- *Stay on top of industry trends.* Even when the economy is booming, some sectors may be in trouble. Your budget should reflect realities in your own industry.

- *Steep yourself in company values.* Every company has values, sometimes formalized and sometimes just "the way we do things around here." Savvy managers factor those values into their decisions. Say your budget calls for layoffs. If the company views layoffs as counterproductive, your proposal will be dead on arrival.

- *Conduct **SWOT analyses**.* What are your company's strengths, weaknesses, opportunities, and threats? Keep them in mind as you build your budget.

All these techniques should help you understand the context in which you'll develop your budget.

Top-down versus bottom-up budgeting

In **top-down budgeting**, senior management sets specific goals for such items as net income, profit margins, and expenses. Each department may be told, for example, to limit expense increases to 6% above the previous year's levels. As you prepare your budget, observe such parameters and look at the company's overall plans for sales and marketing and for costs and expenses. Those objectives provide the framework within which you must operate. For instance, many companies strive to improve profitability every year by reducing expenses as a percentage of revenue.

In **bottom-up budgeting**, managers aren't given specific targets. Instead, they put together budgets that they feel will meet the strategic needs and goals of their respective departments. These budgets are "rolled up" into an overall company budget. The company budget is then adjusted, with requests for changes sent back down to individual departments.

This process can go through multiple iterations. Often it means working closely with departments that may be competing against yours for limited resources. It's good to be as cooperative as you can during this process, but don't hesitate to lobby aggressively for your own unit's needs.

Getting started

Budgets should be ambitious but realistic. Don't map out a budget that you can't meet—but don't underestimate the possibilities. Here's how to begin.

First, list three to five goals that you hope to achieve during the period for which you are budgeting. For example:

- Increase gross sales by 5%.

- Decrease administrative costs as a percentage of revenue by 3 points.

- Reduce inventories by 2% by the end of the fiscal year.

Make sure those goals line up with the organization's strategic priorities.

Next, figure out how you'll achieve them. (Remember that a budget is just a plan with numbers.) How can you generate more revenue? Will you need more sales representatives? Where can you cut costs or reduce inventories?

The smaller the unit you're focusing on, the more detail you need. If you're creating a budget for a 12-person sales office, you typically won't have to worry about capital expenditures such as major upgrades to the building. But you should include detailed estimates for travel costs, telephones and utilities, and office supplies. As you move up in the organization, the scope of your budget will broaden. You can assume that the head of the 12-person office has thought about printer cartridges and gasoline for the sales reps' cars. Your job now is to look at big-picture items such as computer systems and to determine how all the smaller-scale budgets fit together.

Other issues to consider when you're preparing a budget:

- *Term.* Is the budget just for this year, or is it for the next five years? Most budgets apply only to the upcoming year and are reviewed every month or every quarter.

- *Assumptions.* At its simplest, a budget creates projections by adding assumptions to current data. Look hard at the assumptions you're making. Let's suppose you think sales will rise by 10% in the coming year if you add two more people to your unit. Explain what you're basing that assumption on, and show a clear connection to at least one strategic goal (in this case, it's probably to increase sales by a certain percentage).

Role-playing may help you here. Put yourself in the position of a division manager with limited resources and many requests for funding: Under those circumstances, what would persuade *you* to grant a request for two additional staff members?

Articulating your assumptions

Usually, budgeters take the previous year's budget as a starting point. If you're the manager of Amalgamated Hat Rack's Moose Head Division, for instance, you

STEPS FOR CREATING A BUDGET

1. Analyze your company's overall strategy.

2. If your company does top-down budgeting, start with the targets given to you by senior management. If it does bottom-up budgeting, create targets yourself.

3. Articulate your assumptions.

4. Quantify your assumptions.

5. Review: Do the numbers add up? Is your budget defensible in light of the company's strategic goals?

might look at the 2013 budget to get ideas about how to increase revenue, cut costs, or both. (See figure 4, "Moose Head Division, Amalgamated Hat Rack." Note that the parentheses in the table indicate unfavorable variances.)

FIGURE 4

Moose Head Division, Amalgamated Hat Rack

2013 Budget	Budgeted	Actual	Variance
SALES BY MODEL			
Moose Antler Deluxe	$ 237,000	$ 208,560	$ (28,440)
Moose Antler Standard	320,225	329,832	9,607
Standard Upright	437,525	476,902	39,377
Electro-Revolving	125,000	81,250	(43,750)
Hall/Wall	80,000	70,400	(9,600)
Total sales	**$ 1,199,750**	**$ 1,166,944**	**$ (32,806)**
COST OF GOODS SOLD			
Direct labor	$ 75,925	$ 82,000	$ (6,075)
Factory overhead	5,694	6,150	(456)
Direct materials	195,000	191,100	3,900
Total cost of goods sold	**$ 276,619**	**$ 279,250**	**$ (2,631)**
SALES, GENERAL, AND ADMINISTRATIVE COSTS			
Sales salaries	$ 300,00	$ 310,000	$ (10,000)
Advertising expenses	135,000	140,000	(5,000)
Miscellaneous selling expenses	3,400	2,500	900
Office expenses	88,000	90,000	(2,000)
Total SG&A	**$ 526,400**	**$ 542,500**	**$ (16,100)**
Operating income	**$ 396,731**	**$ 345,194**	**$ (51,537)**

TIP: TRACK YOUR THOUGHT PROCESS

As you put your budget into the required format, document your assumptions. It's easy to lose track of them during the budgeting process, and you'll need to explain them—and revise them.

Don't look only at specific revenue or cost line items, because revenue and costs are closely linked. Instead, ask yourself what the budget shows about last year's operations. As the table shows, the Standard Upright and the Moose Antler Standard exceeded sales expectations in 2013. Perhaps it would make sense to increase your sales projections for those products, particularly if your sales reps are optimistic about the prospects for more sales. The Standard Upright might be a particularly good choice, since it beat its 2013 projection by 9%. Could you increase the anticipated sales for this model by 5% or 10% in

2014? How much more would you have to spend on sales or marketing to achieve this increase? To make the decision, you'll need as much data as you can get about pricing, competitors, new sales channels, and other relevant issues.

Alternatively, you might plan to eliminate some products. The Electro-Revolving model, for example, is faring poorly. Would it be better to cut this line and promote the newer Hall/Wall model? That would eliminate $81,250 in sales, but the Electro-Revolving is expensive to produce, so discontinuation might not have much impact on the bottom line.

Other questions to ask yourself:

- Will you keep prices the same, lower them, or raise them? A price increase of 3% might offset the budget's 2013 sales shortfall, provided that it doesn't dampen demand.

- Do you plan to enter new markets, target new customers, or use new sales strategies? How much additional revenue do you expect these efforts to bring in? How much will these initiatives cost?

- Will your cost of goods change? For example, perhaps you plan to cut down on temporary help and add full-time employees in the plant. Or perhaps you hope to reduce wage costs through automation. If so, how much will it cost to automate?

- Are your suppliers likely to raise or lower prices? Are you planning to switch to lower-cost suppliers? Will quality suffer as a result? If so, how much will that affect your sales?

- Do you need to enhance your product to keep your current customers?

- Does your staff need further training?

- Are you planning to pursue other special projects or initiatives?

Articulating your answers to questions like these ensures that your assumptions won't go unexamined. It will help you create budget numbers that are as realistic as possible.

Quantifying your assumptions

Now you need to translate your assumptions and scenarios into dollar figures. Begin with last year's budget and make the changes that fit your plans. If your entire staff of 12 needs sales training, for instance, find out how much the training will cost and add in that amount. Ask your coworkers for their ideas about costs as well. And consult the websites of trade associations or trade publications for data on industry averages.

Because your budget must be compared and combined with others in the organization, your company will probably provide you with a standard set of line items. When you've filled those in, take a step back:

BUDGETING BEST PRACTICES

- *Focus on the main goal.* If it's to increase sales, make that the overriding concern of your budget. Don't let other issues sidetrack you.

- *Be realistic.* Most managers would like to double sales or cut expenses in half. But remember: You'll be held accountable for the results.

- *Get help.* Include your team members; they may have detailed knowledge about certain line items that you don't. Your finance department can help, too.

- *Talk to your staff.* Don't use the budget as a substitute for regular communication with your staff. Team members should hear directly from you about funding for line items that affect them.

Does this budget meet your unit's goals? It's easy to overlook big-picture goals as you get into line-by-line details. Is your budget defensible? You may be perfectly happy with it, but you'll need to win over the budget committee. Once again, push your assumptions. Could you do with one extra staff member instead of two? If not, be sure you can make a good argument as to why not.

Calculating Return on Investment

Calculating Return
on Investment

I magine that Amalgamated Hat Rack is considering two investment options: buying a new piece
of machinery and creating a new product line.
The new machine is a plastic extruder with a price
tag of $100,000. Amalgamated hopes it will save time
and money over the long term, and that it will be safer
than the current equipment. The second possibility,
launching a line of coatracks, will require a $250,000
investment in design, production equipment, and
marketing.

How will Amalgamated decide whether these options make economic sense? And if it can afford only
one of them, how will it decide which to choose?

By figuring out the **return on investment**, or ROI. This means evaluating how much money the investment will generate compared with its cost.

Before you begin any ROI analysis, it's important to understand the costs and benefits of the status quo. You want to weigh the relative merits of each investment against the consequences, if any, of not proceeding with it. Don't assume that the costs of doing nothing are always high. Even if the new investment promises a significant benefit, it still carries risk. The short-term cost—and the short-term risk—of doing nothing is usually close to zero. Of course, the benefits, too, are close to zero.

Costs and benefits

ROI calculations always involve the following steps:

1. Identify all the costs of the new purchase or business opportunity.

2. Estimate the savings to be realized.

3. Estimate how much cash the proposed investment will generate.

4. Map out a time line for expected costs, savings, and cash flows, and use sensitivity analysis to challenge your assumptions.

5. Evaluate the unquantifiable costs and benefits.

The first three steps are fairly straightforward in theory, though they may be complicated in practice. When calculating the costs of an investment, you include up-front costs (the purchase price of a machine, say) and also costs to be incurred in subsequent years (maintenance and upgrades for the new machine). Savings may come from a variety of sources, such as greater throughput per hour, higher quality (and thus less rework), or a decrease in labor requirements. The cash generated typically comes from new sales. If you are calculating the ROI of a marketing campaign, for instance, you will need to estimate the campaign's effect on the company's revenue.

It can be tricky to create a time line for your costs, savings, and increased cash flow, so you may want to turn to your finance department for help with this. Step five is really just a check on the other four: Which costs or benefits can't you quantify, and how will they affect your decision? For example, would a particular investment help or harm your company's reputation in the community or with prospective employees?

Once you have completed these steps, you are ready to use one or more of the analytical tools described in this chapter: payback period, net present value, internal rate of return, break-even analysis, or sensitivity analysis. We'll look at the strengths and weaknesses of each tool to give you a basic understanding. But you may want a colleague from the finance department to assist with the calculations.

Payback period

The **payback period** tells you how long until you recoup your investment. To calculate it, divide the initial investment by the average anticipated cash flow or cost savings per year. For instance, if a new plastic extruder will cost $100,000 and save Amalgamated $18,000 a year, then the payback period is 5.56 years. (See table 1, "Amalgamated extruder savings.")

Payback analysis is the simplest method for evaluating a prospective investment. It's useful mainly for ruling out options. If the extruder is likely to last only five years, for instance, it's obviously a bad investment, because the payback period is longer than that. But payback analysis does not tell you the rate of return on the investment. It also doesn't take into account the time value of money, because it compares outlays today with cash coming in down the road. (We'll discuss this further in the following section.)

TABLE 1

Amalgamated extruder savings

Year	Savings	Cumulative savings
1	$ 18,000	$ 18,000
2	18,000	36,000
3	18,000	54,000
4	18,000	72,000
5	18,000	90,000
6	18,000	108,000
7	18,000	126,000

Net present value and internal rate of return

Net present value (NPV) and **internal rate of return** (IRR) are highly valuable analytical tools, but they can be fairly complex. Because most calculators and spreadsheet programs can do the calculations for you, we'll describe these tools in broad terms only.

Consider the principle that underlies both methods: the time value of money. This principle states that a dollar you receive today is worth more than a dollar you expect to receive in the future. The reason: Even forgetting about inflation, you can spend or invest today's dollar right away. You can't do that with a future dollar. And every dollar you expect in the future comes with some degree of risk. For example, the person or institution that promised it to you may be unable to pay when the time comes.

But you can't evaluate a new business opportunity without figuring out the value of the money you expect it to generate. So you need a method for expressing future dollars in terms of current dollars. That's what NPV and IRR calculations allow you to do.

Suppose that Amalgamated expects a new line of coatracks to generate $60,000 in cash annually, beginning one year from now and continuing for five years. Here are the key questions to consider: Given this anticipated cash flow and the $250,000 in upfront costs, is a new line of coatracks the most productive way to invest that $250,000? Or would

Amalgamated be better off investing its money in the extruder or something else?

Net present value

A net present value calculation *discounts* the anticipated $300,000 in cash flow to accurately express its value in today's dollars. How much should it be discounted? Companies usually establish a minimum rate of return, or **hurdle rate**, that they can reasonably expect to earn on their investments. (The rate is always well above whatever they would earn on relatively low-risk investments such as government bonds.) Let's say that Amalgamated's chief financial officer has set the hurdle rate at 6%.

So your initial outlay is $250,000, the expected return is $60,000 a year for five years, and the discount rate is 6%. If you punch these numbers into the NPV function on your calculator or spreadsheet, the program will give you the NPV. If it's a positive number—

and if no other investments are under consideration—the company should pursue the investment. The NPV for a line of Amalgamated coatracks is $2,742, which suggests that it would be an attractive investment.

But what about the other investment Amalgamated is considering—the $100,000 plastic extruder? At a discount rate of 6% and a savings of $18,000 a year for seven years, its NPV is about $483, which is just barely positive. When we compare NPVs for the two investments, we see that both are positive, but the one for the coatracks is larger. If Amalgamated can afford only one of these investments, it should go with the new line of coatracks.

The discount rate you use makes a big difference in NPV calculations. Suppose the rate were 10% instead of 6%. The NPV for the extruder would then be –$12,368, turning a modestly attractive investment into a very poor one.

Internal rate of return

IRR is based on the same formula as NPV, with one difference: When calculating NPV, you know the desired rate of return—that's the discount rate—and you use it to determine how much money your future cash flows are worth today. With IRR, you essentially set the net present value at zero and solve the equation for the *actual* rate of return. Your spreadsheet program or calculator will also perform IRR calculations for you. If the IRR is greater than the company's hurdle rate, the investment is probably a good bet, though you still need to compare it with other options.

What, then, is a reasonable rate of return for Amalgamated Hat Rack to expect on the new line of coatracks? According to the IRR calculation, it's 6.4%, which is slightly above the discount rate. So this is a good investment. But again, it wouldn't be if the hurdle rate were 10%.

Break-even analysis

Break-even analysis is useful when an investment you're considering will enable you to sell something new or sell more of something you already offer. It tells you how much (or how much more) you need to sell in order to pay for the fixed investment—in other words, at what point you will break even. With that information in hand, you can look at market demand and competitors' market shares to determine whether selling that much is realistic.

First let's put the goal in more precise terms. We're trying to determine the volume at which the incremental contribution from a product line equals the total cost of your investment. "Contribution" in this context means the revenue you get from each unit sold minus that unit's variable costs. **Variable costs** include the cost of materials and any direct labor involved in producing the unit.

Here are the steps:

- Subtract the variable cost per unit from the unit revenue. This is the unit contribution.

- Divide your total investment by the unit contribution.

The quotient is the break-even volume, expressed as the number of units (or additional units) that must be sold to cover the cost of the investment.

Suppose the new coatracks sell for $75 each, and the variable cost per unit is $22. The figure "Break-even calculation" shows how to determine the break-even volume for the coatracks.

At this point, Amalgamated must decide whether the break-even volume is achievable. Can it reasonably expect to sell more than 4,717 units? If so, how quickly? What will it take to make that happen?

To calculate the break-even volume for the extruder, you would define the unit contribution as the

FIGURE 5

Break-even calculation

$ 75   (unit revenue)
−22   (variable cost per unit)
─────────────────────
$53   (unit contribution)

$ 250,000   (total investment required)
÷ 53   (unit contribution)
─────────────────────
4,717 coatracks (break-even volume)

savings per unit. If the new extruder will save $10 per unit, then your break-even volume is $100,000 divided by $10, or 10,000 units.

Sensitivity analysis

As noted, Amalgamated expects its new line of coatracks to begin generating $60,000 in annual cash flow a year from now. But what if some variable in the scenario changed? How would it affect your evaluation of the investment opportunity? Sensitivity analysis enables you to see what changes in your assumptions might mean.

Imagine that people within Amalgamated disagree about the prospects for the new line of coatracks. Sherman Peabody is the vice president of Amalgamated's Moose Head Division. He would exercise day-to-day oversight of the new product line, and he is the one projecting $60,000 in annual cash flow for five years. Natasha Rubskaya, the company's CFO, is more doubtful about the investment, primarily because she believes that Peabody has drastically underestimated the marketing costs necessary to support the new line. She predicts an annual cash flow of only $45,000. Then there's Theodore Bullmoose, Amalgamated's senior vice president for new business development. Ever the optimist, he is convinced that the coatracks will practically sell themselves, generating an annual cash flow of $75,000 a year.

So Amalgamated conducts a sensitivity analysis using the three scenarios. The NPV for Peabody's is $2,742. For Rubskaya's, it's -$60,444. For Bullmoose's, it's $65,927.

If Rubskaya is right, the coatracks won't be worth the investment. If either of the other two is right, the investment will pay off, with a reasonable amount according to Peabody's profit projections and a generous amount according to Bullmoose's. Here is where judgment comes into play. If Rubskaya has shown herself to be the most reliable estimator of the three, Amalgamated's CEO might accept her projection of the new line's potential. But whichever route the CEO takes, the sensitivity analysis provides a more nuanced view of the investment and how it would be affected by various changes in assumptions. Changes in other variables can be mapped out just as easily.

Evaluating unquantifiable costs and benefits

The numbers never tell the whole story, so your ROI analysis should acknowledge qualitative factors as well. Does the new opportunity fit with the company's mission? Can the management team take on a new product line without losing focus? At times, seemingly unquantifiable factors can at least be estimated numerically. Suppose you're evaluating an investment in a new database, and you are trying to assess the value of the information it will provide. You might come up with a ballpark dollar figure representing the value of employees' time saved. You might also estimate the value of increased customer retention due to better understanding of purchase patterns. You may or may not decide to incorporate such estimates into your ROI calculations, but they can be helpful when you make the case for the investment.

Tracking
Performance

Tracking Performance

W hen you prepare a budget or decide on an investment, you can be certain of one thing: The numbers will not be exactly as you predicted. That's why you need to monitor your results. If they differ significantly from your projections, you can take corrective action. If they are more or less on track, you can be confident that you are in control of the situation.

Performance of an investment

When you evaluate a new investment, you're planning for the long term—typically a year or more. But if you track your projections monthly, you'll spot variations early.

Consider Amalgamated's new Coatrack Division. The senior team ended up using Theodore Bull-moose's optimistic cash flow projection of $75,000 a year (or $6,250 a month) as the basis for its investment. Table 2, "Amalgamated Hat Rack, Coatrack Division, January 2013 results," shows the state of affairs early in the first quarter. (For simplicity's sake, we'll assume here that operating profit is equivalent to the cash flow projections used for NPV calculations.)

The division is doing reasonably well on revenue and cost of goods sold. Its most significant negative variance is in the marketing expense line. It's difficult to be certain on the basis of figures from just the first month: Is this simply a onetime or seasonal variation? Or will Amalgamated have to spend more on marketing than anticipated?

If your ROI varies from what you expected—and the pattern of unexpectedly high costs (or unexpect-

TABLE 2

Amalgamated Hat Rack, Coatrack Division, January 2013 results

Item	Budget January	Actual January	Variance
Coatrack revenue	$ 39,000	$ 38,725	$ (275)
Cost of goods sold	19,500	19,200	300
Gross profit	19,500	19,575	25
Marketing	8,500	10,100	(1,600)
Administrative expenses	4,750	4,320	430
Total operating expenses	13,250	14,420	(1,170)
Operating profit	**$ 6,250**	**$ 5,105**	**$ (1,145)**

edly low revenue) seems likely to hold—it may be necessary to correct course. Amalgamated might decide to reduce its marketing outlay. Or it might decide to keep spending at that level, recalculate the expected cash flow, and see whether the investment still makes sense. Since Bullmoose's projection was highly optimistic, the company has some wiggle room before it must conclude that it has made a bad investment.

Performance of an existing unit

Tracking the budget for an established unit involves many of the same procedures. You monitor results so that you can make spending or operating adjustments as quickly as possible. When a line item contains a surprise, ask first whether the reason is related to timing. In other words, are you looking at a monthly aberration or a long-term problem?

If you suspect an aberration, don't be too concerned; the situation should straighten itself out. Just keep a close eye on that line item in subsequent months. If the variance is not an aberration, however, you need to determine why it's occurring. Maybe expenses are higher than budgeted because sales have increased sharply, in which case expense overruns would be good news rather than bad. Alternatively, maybe you made a poor projection and must find some way to make up the loss. Can you decrease

TIP: ENLIST HELP WITH ABERRATIONS

Involve team members in addressing variances. They're likely to have some good ideas about what's going on and what to do about it.

spending on other line items to compensate for those that are over budget?

Forecasts

In addition to comparing your actual results to the budget, you'll sit down and update your projections with new information to create forecasts. But don't throw out the old estimates in the process. When budget time rolls around next year, you'll want to assess how accurate your original assumptions were. That will help you improve your estimates the next time around.

If you are well off budget partway into the year—and if your forecasts don't show a correction—let senior management know. Explain the reasons for the variances and how you propose to make up for them. That way, the senior team can adjust the overall company forecast and perhaps provide direction on whether and how to address the shortfalls.

Test Yourself

Test Yourself

Below you'll find 10 multiple-choice questions to help you assess your knowledge of finance and budgeting essentials. Answers appear after the test.

1. **If you want to recognize the costs connected to a sale during the period when the sale was made, which accounting method would you use?**

    a. Accrual accounting
    b. Cash-based accounting

2. **Which of the following would be considered part of cost of goods sold, or COGS?**

   a. Administrative employee salaries
   b. Sales and marketing costs
   c. Rents
   d. Labor costs for assembling the product
   e. Advertising costs

3. **In most accounting systems, short-term or current liabilities are those that must be paid in less than:**

   a. One month
   b. Three months
   c. One year

4. **If the income statement can tell you whether a company is making a profit, what does the cash flow statement tell you?**

   a. How efficiently a company is using its assets

b. Whether a company is turning profits into cash

c. How well a company is managing its liabilities

5. **Many analysts like to look at a ratio that shows how profitable a company's operating activities are. Which ratio shows this?**

a. Acid-test ratio
b. Accounts receivable
c. EBIT margin

6. **At ABC Company, unit heads develop budgets for their departments that are linked to company performance objectives. Is this top-down or bottom-up budgeting?**

a. Top-down
b. Bottom-up

7. **As you begin to prepare your unit's budget, your manager reminds you to be aware of the "scope" of your budget. What does "scope" mean?**

   a. The context of the proposed budget: the three to five goals it aims to achieve.

   b. The part of the company the budget is supposed to cover and the level of detail it should include.

   c. Whether the budget includes revenue and profits as well as the operating costs of your unit.

8. **When you're analyzing ROI, payback period analysis can help you rule out bad investments. What is the main drawback of this method?**

   a. It ignores the time value of money.

   b. It does not tell you how long it will take for the investment to break even.

   c. It can be used only to evaluate potential capital investments, not other types of new business opportunities.

9. **Your company is considering making an investment that could enable your division to sell more units of new tracking software introduced last year. Your manager has asked you to determine how many units the company would need to sell to recoup this investment. What analytical method might help you come up with an answer?**

   a. Break-even analysis
   b. Net present value analysis
   c. Internal rate of return analysis

10. **To track your budget, you carry out three steps on a monthly basis. Step two is missing in the list below; what is it?**

    Step 1. Assess monthly revenue and expense performance.

    Step 2. _____.

Step 3. Determine whether and how your bottom line will be affected by any variances.

a. Assess your company's capital expenditures.
b. Revise your forecast for the coming quarter.
c. Determine positive and negative variances compared with budget.

Answers to test questions

1:   **a.** With accrual accounting, costs are matched to the associated sales, regardless of whether cash is actually received or paid in that period. By matching expenses with revenues in the same time period, accrual accounting helps managers understand how profitable a company's products or services are.

2:   **d.** Assembly labor costs are considered part of COGS. Cost of goods sold includes the materials, labor, and other costs that are directly attributable to manufacturing a product or delivering a service.

3: **c.** Generally, short-term liabilities have to be paid in a year or less. Long-term liabilities stretch out over a longer period and include items such as long-term bonds and mortgages.

4: **b.** The cash flow statement tells you how well a company is turning its profits into cash.

5: **c.** Many analysts use EBIT (earnings before interest and taxes) margin, often known as operating margin, to gauge the profitability of a company's operations.

6: **a.** In top-down budgeting, senior management sets specific performance objectives for individual units. For instance, unit managers may be asked to limit expense growth to no more than 5% over the previous year's expenses. They then develop their budgets within those limits.

7: **b.** Scope entails two things: the part of the company your budget is supposed to cover and the level of detail it should include.

8: **a.** Because payback analysis ignores the time value of money, it does not provide as accurate an economic picture as more sophisticated tools, such as net present value and internal rate of return.

9: **a.** Break-even analysis tells you how much (or how much more) of a product you need to sell in order to pay for a fixed investment—in other words, at what point you will break even financially. You can then use your sales history and knowledge of the market to determine whether the break-even volume is realistic.

10: **c.** Step two is to compare budgeted figures with actuals and calculate variances. You can then determine to what extent these variances will affect your bottom line.

Key Terms

Accounts payable (A/P). Money owed by a company to suppliers.

Accounts receivable (A/R). Money owed to a company for goods or services sold.

Accrual. An amount incurred as an expense in a given accounting period but not paid by the end of that period.

Accrual accounting. An accounting method whereby revenue and expenses are booked when they are incurred, regardless of when they are actually received or paid. Revenue is recognized in the time period when the goods or services are delivered; expenses are recognized in the same period as their associated revenues.

Acid-test ratio. See *quick ratio.*

Allocation. The process of dividing costs in a certain category among several cost centers, typically on the basis of usage. For example, corporate overhead such as rent and utilities may be allocated to departments according to the number of square feet they occupy.

Amortization. A charge on the income statement reflecting a portion of the cost of an intangible asset such as a patent.

Assets. The economic resources of a company. Assets include cash, accounts receivable, inventories, land, buildings, vehicles, machinery, equipment, and other investments.

Asset turnover. A measure of how efficiently a company uses its assets. To calculate, divide sales by assets. In general, the higher the number, the better.

Balance sheet. A document summarizing a company's financial position—its assets, liabilities, and owners' equity—at a specific point in time. According to the fundamental equation of the balance sheet, a company's assets equal its liabilities plus owners' equity.

Banker's ratio. See *current ratio.*

Book value. The value at which an asset is carried on a balance sheet. The book value of a new asset is its purchase price, but that figure is reduced each year for depreciation. So the asset's book value at any point in time is its cost minus accumulated depreciation.

Bottom-up budgeting. A process whereby managers put together budgets that they feel will best meet the needs and goals of their respective departments or units. These budgets are "rolled up" to create an overall company budget, which is then adjusted, with requests for changes being sent back down to the individual departments.

Breakeven. The volume at which the total contribution from a product line equals total fixed costs. To calculate it, subtract the variable cost per unit from the selling price to determine the unit contribution; then divide total fixed costs by the unit contribution. Breakeven on an investment is the point when the net cash received from the investment equals its cost.

Capital expenditure or capital investment. Payment to acquire or improve a capital asset.

Cash-based accounting. The recording of revenue and expenses when cash actually changes hands. This approach is seldom used except by very small companies.

Cash flow statement. A statement showing whcre the company's cash comes from and where it goes.

Contributed capital. Capital funds received in exchange for stock.

Contributiun. In product cost analysis, unit revenue minus variable cost per unit; the sum of money available to contribute to fixed costs.

Cost of capital. The percentage rate a company must pay investors or lenders in return for its capital funding. Companies calculate their *weighted average cost of capital* by taking into account factors such as the average interest rate on their debt, the expected rate of return on their equity, and their tax rate.

Cost of goods sold (COGS). Costs directly associated with making a product.

Cost of services (COS). Costs directly associated with delivering a service.

Current assets. Those assets that are most easily converted into cash, including cash on hand, accounts receivable, and inventory.

Current ratio. A comparison of a company's current assets with its current liabilities. To calculate, divide total current assets by total current liabilities.

Days payable outstanding. A measure indicating how many days it takes, on average, for a company to pay its suppliers. To calculate, divide accounts payable by cost of goods sold per day.

Days sales outstanding. A measure indicating how long it takes, on average, for a company to collect its receivables. To calculate, divide accounts receivable by revenue per day.

Debt. Money owed to a creditor.

Debt-to-equity ratio. A comparison of a company's outstanding loans to its owners' equity. To calculate the debt-to-equity ratio, divide total liabilities by owners' equity.

Depreciation. A charge on the income statement representing a portion of the cost of a tangible asset such as a building or a machine. The cost of such assets is charged over their estimated useful life.

Direct costs. Costs directly attributable to the manufacture of a product or the delivery of a service—for example, the cost of plastic for a bottle manufacturer or the cost of a service technician's time for a copier service company.

Dividend. A payment (usually issued quarterly) to the stockholders of a company, as a return on their investment.

Earnings before interest and taxes (EBIT). See *operating profit*.

Earnings per share (EPS). A company's net income divided by the number of shares outstanding. One of the most common indicators of a public company's financial performance.

Earnings statement. See *income statement*.

Economic Value Added (EVA). Net income minus a charge for the cost of a company's capital.

Efficiency ratios. Financial measures that link various income statement and balance sheet figures to gauge a company's operating efficiency. Examples include asset turnover, days sales outstanding, days payable outstanding, and inventory days.

Equity. The value of a company's assets minus its liabilities. On a balance sheet, equity is referred to as shareholders' equity or owners' equity.

Financial leverage. The extent to which a company's assets are financed by debt. A company that has a high debt-to-equity ratio (by industry standards) is said to be highly leveraged.

Financial statements   Reports of a company's financial performance. The three fundamental statements are the income statement, the balance sheet, and the cash flow statement; they present related information but provide different perspectives on performance.

Fiscal period or reporting period. An accounting time period (usually a month, a quarter, or a year) at the end of which the books are closed and profit or loss is determined.

Fixed assets. Assets that are difficult to convert to cash, such as buildings and equipment.

Fixed costs. Costs that remain constant in the short run regardless of sales volume; they include administrative salaries, interest, rent, and insurance.

Generally accepted accounting principles (GAAP). The rules and conventions that accountants in the United States follow when recording and summarizing transactions and preparing financial statements.

Gross margin. Gross profit as a percentage of revenue.

Gross profit. The sum remaining when COGS is subtracted from revenue.

Growth. An increase in the company's revenue, profits, or owners' equity.

Hurdle rate. A company's minimum required rate of return on its investments.

Income statement. A report showing a company's revenue, expenses, and profit over a period of time, usually a month, a quarter, or a year. The income statement is also known as a profit-and-loss statement

(P&L), a statement of operations, and a statement of earnings.

Indirect costs. Costs not directly attributable to the manufacture of a product or the provision of a service.

Interest coverage. An indicator of a company's margin of safety on its interest costs—specifically, how many times over the company could make its interest payments out of current operating profits. To calculate interest coverage, divide EBIT by interest expense.

Internal rate of return (IRR). The rate at which the net present value (NPV) of an investment equals zero.

Inventory. Material that will eventually be fabricated and/or sold. Examples include the merchandise in a shop, finished goods in a warehouse, work in progress, and raw materials.

Inventory days. A measure of how long it takes a company to sell the average amount of inventory on hand during a given period of time. To calculate inventory days, divide average inventory by cost of goods sold per day.

Invoice. A bill submitted to a purchaser for goods or services rendered.

Leverage ratios. Ratios related to a company's use of debt. They include interest coverage and debt to equity, and help people assess a company's ability to pay what it owes.

Liabilities. The financial claims against a company's resources, including accounts payable, loans, and mortgages.

Net income. An organization's profit after all expenses, including interest and taxes, are subtracted from revenue.

Net present value (NPV). The estimated current value of an investment, calculated by subtracting the cost of the investment from the present value of the investment's future earnings.

Net profit margin. See *return on sales*.

Operating cash flow (OCF). The net movement of cash from the operations side of a business, as opposed to cash related to investments or to a company's financing.

Operating expenses. Expenses that are not directly attributed to manufacturing a product or delivering a service—for example, administrative salaries, rents, and sales and marketing costs.

Operating profit. The sum remaining after all operating costs are subtracted from revenue. Also known as earnings before interest and taxes (EBIT).

Owners' equity. See *equity*.

Payback period. The length of time needed to recoup the cost of a capital investment.

Pretax profit. Net income before income taxes.

Price-to-book ratio. A ratio comparing the market's valuation of a company to the value of that company as indicated by its owners' equity.

Price-to-earnings ratio (P/E). The current price of a share of stock divided by the previous 12 months' earnings per share. This ratio helps you compare stocks' value.

Productivity measures. Indicators—such as sales per employee and net income per employee—that link revenue and profit information to workforce data.

Profitability ratios. Measures of a company's level of profitability, in which profits are expressed as a percentage of various other items. Examples include return on assets, return on equity, and return on sales.

Property, plant, and equipment (PPE). A line on the balance sheet indicating how much money (after depreciation) a company has invested in fixed assets such as buildings and machinery.

Quick ratio. A measure of a company's ability to meet its short-term obligations, also known as the *acid test*. To calculate the quick ratio, divide cash, receivables, and marketable securities by current liabilities.

Ratio analysis. A means of analyzing the information contained in the three financial statements. A financial ratio is two key numbers from a company's financial statements expressed in relation to each other.

Retained earnings. All after-tax income held by a business (and not paid out in dividends) since its inception.

Return on assets (ROA). A measure of the productivity of a company's assets. To calculate ROA, divide net income by total assets.

Return on equity (ROE). A measure of the productivity of a company's equity. Also known as return on owners' equity. To calculate ROE, divide net income by owners' equity.

Return on sales (ROS). A measure of a company's overall efficiency in generating profits. Also known as net profit margin. To calculate ROS, divide net income by total sales.

Revenue. The first line on an income statement, indicating the value of goods or services delivered to customers during the period of time covered by the statement. Also called *sales*.

Sales. An exchange of goods and services for money. (See *revenue*.)

Shareholders' equity. See *equity*.

SWOT analysis. An analysis of a company's strengths, weaknesses, opportunities, and threats.

Time value of money. The principle that a dollar received today is worth more than a dollar expected at some point in the future.

Top-down budgeting. A process whereby senior management sets specific objectives for items such as net income, profit margin, and expenses. Unit managers then put together their budgets within these parameters.

Valuation. An estimate of a company's value for the purposes of purchase, sale, or investment.

Variable costs. Costs that vary according to sales volume, such as the cost of materials and sales commissions.

Working capital. A measure of a company's day-to-day liquidity. Working capital equals the difference between a company's current assets and its current liabilities.

Learn More

We recommend:

Berman, Karen, and Joe Knight, with John Case. *Financial Intelligence: A Manager's Guide to Knowing What the Numbers Really Mean*. revised ed. Boston: Harvard Business Review Press, 2013.

In *Financial Intelligence*, Berman and Knight teach the basics of finance—but with a twist. Financial reporting, they argue, is as much art as science. Because nobody can quantify everything, accountants always rely on estimates, assumptions, and judgment calls. Savvy managers need to know how those sources of possible bias can affect the financials. While providing the foundation for a deep understanding of the financial side of business, the book also arms managers with practical strategies for improving their companies' performance—strategies (such as managing the balance sheet) that are well understood by financial professionals but rarely shared with their nonfinancial colleagues.

Harvard Business School Publishing. *HBR Guide to Finance Basics for Managers*. Boston: Harvard Business Review Press, 2012.

This installment in the HBR Guide series explains financial statements and shows how to use the information they contain to make better business decisions. Among the topics covered: growing profits by streamlining your business, working your assets to boost growth, understanding balance sheet levers, and learning to speak the language of ROI. The book also investigates what the financial statements do *not* tell you, along with the "five traps" of performance measurement.

The following works (organized in reverse chronological order) may also be helpful:

Mason, Roger. *Finance for Non-Financial Managers in a Week: A Teach Yourself Guide.* New York: McGraw-Hill, 2012.

Matias, Anthony J. *Budgeting and Forecasting: The Quick Reference Handbook.* Cambridge, MA: Matias & Associates, 2012.

Shoffner, H. George, Susan Shelly, and Robert A. Cooke. *The McGraw-Hill 36-Hour Course: Finance for Non-Financial Managers.* 3rd ed. New York: McGraw-Hill, 2011.

Fields, Edward. *The Essentials of Finance and Accounting for Nonfinancial Managers.* 2nd ed. New York: Amacom Books, 2011.

Weaver, Samuel C., and J. Fred Weston. *Finance and Accounting for Nonfinancial Managers.* New York: McGraw-Hill, 2004.

Siciliano, Gene. *Finance for Non-Financial Managers. Briefcase Books Series.* New York: McGraw-Hill Briefcase Books, 2003.

Kemp, Sid, and Eric Dunbar. *Budgeting for Managers. Briefcase Books Series.* New York: McGraw-Hill Briefcase Books, 2003.

Sources

Harvard Business School Publishing, Harvard Manage-
  Mentor. Boston: Harvard Business Publishing, 2002.
Harvard Business School Publishing. *HBR Guide to Finance
  Basics for Managers.* Boston: Harvard Business Review
  Press, 2012.
Harvard Business School Publishing. *Pocket Mentor: Under-
  standing Finance.* Boston: Harvard Business School Press,
  2006.

Index

Index

Index

property, plant, and equipment (PPE), 20–21, 113

quick ratio, 37, 113

ratio analysis, 32, 113
  efficiency ratios, 35–36
  leverage ratios, 38–39
  liquidity ratios, 37–38
  profitability ratios, 33–34
recessions, 47–48
reporting period, 107
retained earnings, 22, 114
return on assets (ROA), 33, 114
return on equity (ROE), 34, 114
return on investment (ROI), 65–80
  break-even analysis, 68, 75–77
  costs and benefits in, 66–68
  evaluating unquantifiable costs and benefits, 80
  internal rate of return, 68, 70–71, 74

net present value, 68, 70–74
payback period analysis, 68, 69–70,
sensitivity analysis, 68, 77–79
tracking performance and, 83–85
return on sales (ROS), 33, 114
revenue, 5. *See also* sales
  definition of, 114–115
  in income statements, 14
  matching to costs, 12–13. *See also* accrual accounting
ROI. *See* return on investment (ROI)

sales, 5. *See also* revenue
  days sales outstanding, 35
  definition of, 115
  per employee, 43
  projections, budget development and, 56
  return on, 33
  total net, in income statements, 14

Smarter than the average guide.

Harvard Business Review Guides

If you enjoyed this book and want more comprehensive guidance on essential professional skills, turn to the **HBR Guides series**. Packed with concise, practical tips from leading experts—and examples that make them easy to apply—these books help you master big work challenges with advice from the most trusted brand in business.